THE FANTASTIC FART ACTIVITY BOOK

Hilarious Mazes, Word Searches, Code Breakers, and Puzzles for
FLATULENT FUN!

Sky Pony Press books may be purchased in bulk at special discounts for sales promotion, corporate gifts, fund-raising, or educational purposes. Special editions can also be created to specifications. For details, contact the Special Sales Department, Sky Pony Press, 307 West 36th Street, 11th Floor, New York, NY 10018 or info@skyhorsepublishing.com.

Sky Pony® is a registered trademark of Skyhorse Publishing, Inc.®, a Delaware corporation.

Visit our website at www.skyponypress.com.

10 9 8 7 6 5 4 3 2 1

Library of Congress Cataloging-in-Publication Data is available on file.

Design by Melissa Gerber

ISBN: 978-1-5107-7111-6

Printed in China

THE FANTASTIC FART ACTIVITY BOOK

Hilarious Mazes, Word Searches,
Code Breakers, and Puzzles for

>- FLATULENT FUN! -<

BRIAN BOONE

Sky Pony Press
New York

FIND THE FARTS

Can you find all the fun ways to say FART in the word search below?

```
F L U F F Y T R Y T R F F I H W B
R E K N O H P R E E N Y F X Y T B
R P D K U N P L S S N J X L E M P
R V O R K M K S K L E B X I O O T
E W P O R D I L J D L E S G O O D
L N J T T H N V B R S T H F Z M F
G R X G J I J M E T O V T C S Y Z
R T S A L B E T E O T T V T K D N
U R P Q N X T A T X M P I B L A T
G D G R U I M M R Q X N M B L R L
T M W K L E C G T E K Q B U I D G
M T J P R R A K K E D U U P R Z D
B R S B A J J K R D B I P A X F L
J R B C K X R N E B J E L M K Z R
D L K X Q G T R L R R T S X E M
J Z V Y J T R E N J K Q V J N Y R
Y J Z R J V R P X R N Q L D B L Y
```

Whiff	Splitter	Hisser	Floof
Tootsie	Slider	Gurgler	Pootie
Thurp	Ripper	Frump	Crack
Stinker	Quaker	Fluffy	Blat
Steamer	Poof	Cheeser	Blast
Squeaker	Honker	Bubbler	

SQUARED UP: STINKY STUFF

Each of four fart-related images can appear just once in each row, each column, and each 4-box diagonal. Fill in the remaining empty boxes with your own drawings of each of the four fart-y things.

fART REBUS

This puzzle is called a *rebus*. To solve it, identify the word suggested by each image, then put all the words together to form a question you might ask when you smell something bad in a crowded elevator.

-en

+

?

6

MR. FaRT'S FaNTaSTIC JOURNEY

Can you help Mr. Fart escape the intestine where he was born and race to the fanny . . . and freedom?

BEAN IS THE WORD

No food is more famously flatulent than beans. There are a lot of different kinds of beans, and they all make you fart. But can you fill in this crossword puzzle with the names of a bunch of them?

ACROSS

3. Sounds like the name of a green citrus fruit
7. Pink and named after an organ
11. Opposite of "Bad Southern"
12. Sounds like the name of a face bruise and a vegetable
15. Rhymes with lava
16. Does this bean fight on battleships?

DOWN

1. These beans are the color of night
2. Beans wrapped in a tortilla
4. A color and a word that describes a book you've completed
5. Green and found in a pod
6. A Mexican style of bean preparation
8. A cold side dish made from a trio of beans
9. Rhymes with "dung"
10. Another name for soybeans
13. It starts with the name of a baby bird
14. Sounds like "hint-o"

COLORFUL SCENTS

Color this tooting hedgehog and celebrate
the fact that animals fart, too!

IDENTIFY THE CURSED JAR

Each of these seven jars is holding what looks like air . . .
except that one of them holds the smelliest fart ever known
to humanity. Can you figure out which one of the jars is
the smelliest and should be put on a *very* high shelf?

THE CLUES

1. It's not on the far right.
2. It has another jar above it.
3. It's not an odd-numbered jar.

HOW to Say FaRt WitHOUt SaYiNg FaRt

Connect the dots and color this picture of a Whoopee Cushion doing what it was made to do!

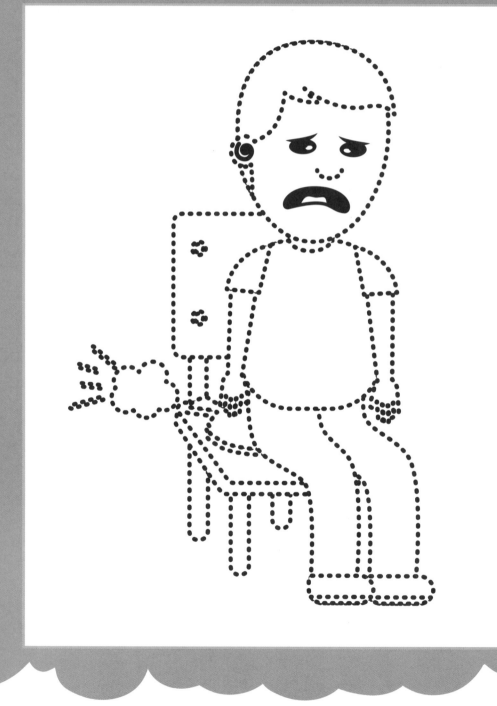

It's a Race: Fart to the Head of the Class

Start at each character's name and work your way down the ladders to discover which kid's fart makes it to the front of the classroom (and to the teacher's nose) first. One thing: Every time you move down to a horizontal (sideways) line, you have to take it over to the next vertical (up and down) line and continue.

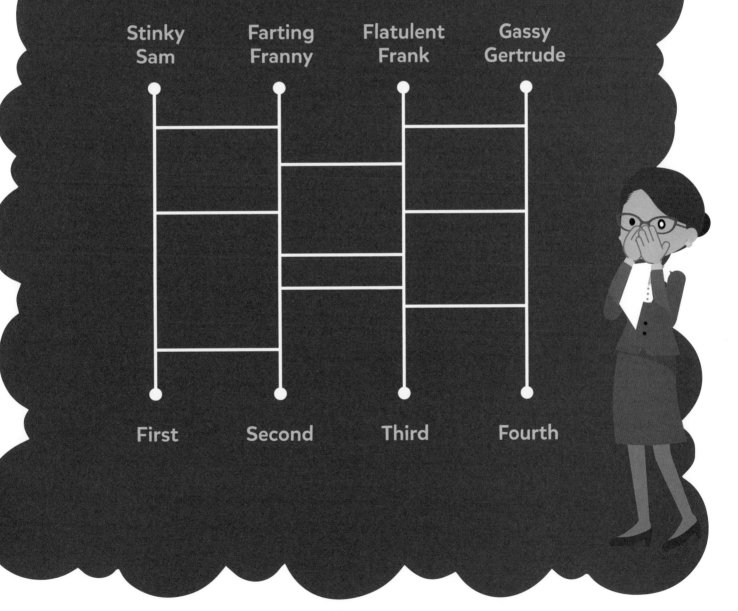

Stinky Sam   Farting Franny   Flatulent Frank   Gassy Gertrude

First   Second   Third   Fourth

Spot the Differences

It looks like this kid is suffering a "fart attack" . . . and so is her *almost* twin. Can you spot six differences between the two pictures?

CRACK THE CODE

In the puzzle below, each number represents a different letter of the alphabet. Based on the few we've given you to get started, figure out the whole alphabet and use it to reveal a fun fact about sneaky farts.

A	B	C	D	E	F	G	H	I	J	K	L	M
			12		19							

N	O	P	Q	R	S	T	U	V	W	X	Y	Z
11	10				4				1			

F A R T S   O   O D
19 18 17 14 4   13 11 15   5 11 24 12

D
22 3   12 15 17 22 3 2   14 5 20

D   S   P
12 18 13   20 4 23 18   10 20

W   O '
1 5 22 24 20   13 11 15 17 20

S   P
4 24 20 20 10 22 3 2

15

SQUARED UP: FART-TASTIC

Each of four fart-based images can appear just once in each row, each column, and each of the four boxes. Fill in the remaining empty boxes with the pictures of each of the four farty things.

READ A-ROUND

Start at the can of baked beans. Write every third letter on the spaces until all have been used. If you place the letters correctly, you'll reveal a fascinating fact about the heft of a fart. Remember to cross out the letters as you go.

TEETSIHO ▲ GRNHEESEFAOABURONTUCW

O__ ____ _____

_____ _____ _____

17

WiNDY ANAGRAMS

The following words and phrases are all anagrams of words associated with breaking wind. Unscramble them, and the bolded boxes will reveal a familiar fart-related sound.

1. SUBPOENA

☐ ☐ ☐ ☐   ☐ ☐ ☐ ☐

2. LATENT FLU

☐ ☐ ☐ ☐ ☐ ☐ ☐ ☐ ☐

3. RAFTS

☐ ☐ ☐ ☐ ☐

4. BARS PRYER

☐ ☐ ☐ ☐ ☐ ☐ ☐ ☐ ☐

5. EAR NERD

☐ ☐ ☐ ☐   ☐ ☐ ☐

6. FAKE CRIB

☐ ☐ ☐ ☐ ☐ ☐ ☐ ☐

7. MR TEASE

☐ ☐ ☐ ☐ ☐ ☐ ☐

MYSTERY WORD:

_ _ _ _ _ _ _ _

18

WORD LADDER

Can you transform a fart-related word into the thing a loud fart does to your dog in just a few steps, changing only one letter each time? Answer the clues to help you get there.

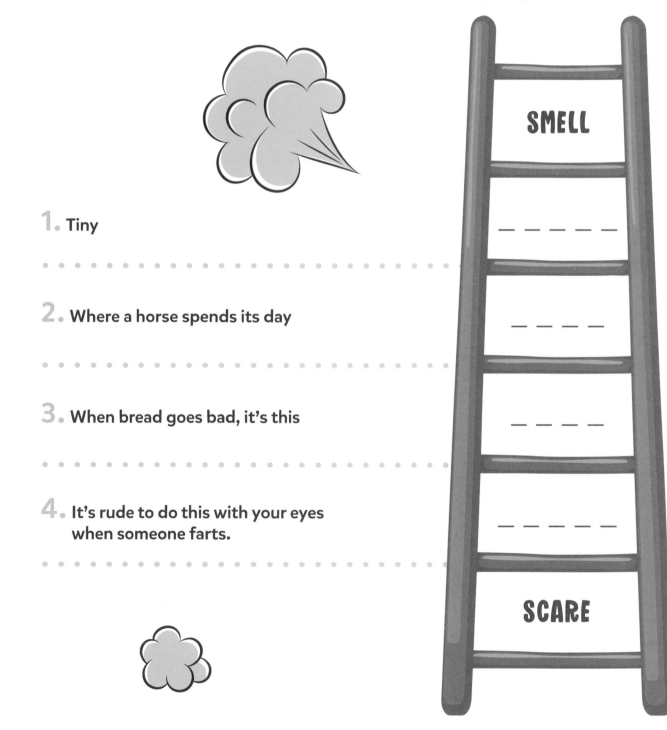

SMELL

1. Tiny

_ _ _ _ _

2. Where a horse spends its day

_ _ _ _ _

3. When bread goes bad, it's this

_ _ _ _ _

4. It's rude to do this with your eyes when someone farts.

_ _ _ _ _

SCARE

COlORfUl SCeNtS

Color the gassy panda as he shoots bamboo-
scented farts into the forest.

NOT LiKe the ReST

Here are eight pictures of a guy farting. They all seem to be the same picture, but take a closer look. One of them is not like the others. Can you find the unique picture?

1.
2.
3.
4.
5.
6.
7.
8.

SAME LETTER CONNECTOR

Boxes connected by lines contain the same letter. We've given you some letters that you can use to fill in some boxes. Others you'll have to figure out on your own. Once all the boxes are filled in, you'll find the answer to this fart joke:

WHAT'S THE DIFFERENCE BETWEEN A HOT TUB AND A REGULAR TUB?

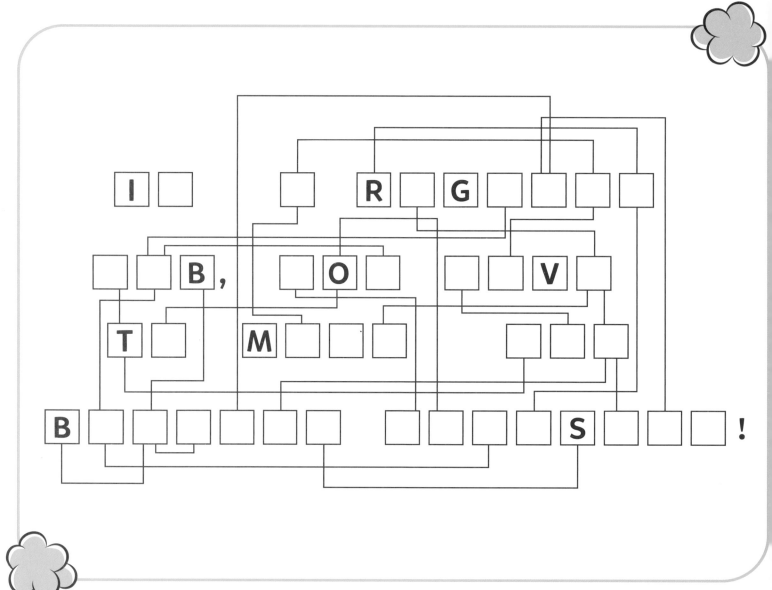

BEFORE, AFTER, IN-BETWEEN

Solve the puzzle to reveal three funny phrases—one said before a fart, one during a fart, and one after a fart. Add a letter to the empty space. Use the letters above and below the spaces, and your expert knowledge of the alphabet, to fill in the correct letter. The first one is done for you. *Note: If you get a Z, the following letter is A.*

1.

P _ _ _   _ _   _ _ _ _ _ _ !

QVMM NZ GJOHFS
RWNN OA HKPIGT

(Answer: PULL MY FINGER!)

2.

SGHR NMD HR RHKDMS ATS CDZCKX

_ _ _ _   _ _ _   _ _   _ _ _ _ _ _   _ _ _   _ _ _ _ _ _ !

UIJT POF JT TJMFOU CVU EFBEMZ

(Answer: THIS ONE IS SILENT BUT DEADLY!)

3.

QMPPW YZMSR RFCEYQ JCYI
RNQQX ZANTS SGDFZR KDZJ

_ _ _ _ _   _ _ _ _ _   _ _ _   _ _ _   _ _ _ _ !

(Answer: SORRY ABOUT THE GAS LEAK!)

COLOR BY CLUE

Add some life to this picture of a farting unicorn when you color by number. Solve the clues to know which number represents which color.

THE CLUES:

1. This color rhymes with mellow, as in "that fart was not mellow."
2. This color sounds like blew, as in "that fart blew right into my nose."
3. This color rhymes with dead, as in "Did you fart or step in a dead thing?"
4. This color rhymes with teen, as in "A teen's farts smell worse than anybody's."
5. This color rhymes with stink, as in "Your farts stink."

PICTURE CROSSWORD

Fill in the blanks by correctly choosing the name of one of the images below. The bolded letter of each will spell out the name of the stinkiest ingredients of a fart.

1. Dropped a __ __ __ __

2. Unleashed a stink __ __ __ __ __ __

3. Played the trouser __ __ __ __ __ __ __

4. Cut the __ __ __ __ __

5. Released some __ __ __

6. Broke __ __ __ __

7. Made a one-gun __ __ __ __ __ __ __

The stinkiest ingredient in a fart is:

__ __ __ __ __ __ __

COLORFUL SCENTS

Color this fox who's caught in the act—and proud of it!

BaD DOG!

One of these five dogs just let loose an especially foul-smelling fart. Using the clues below, can you solve this flatulent mystery and determine which dog needs to start eating a different kind of food?

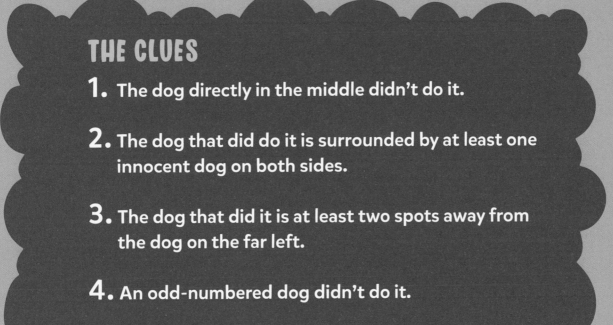

THE CLUES

1. The dog directly in the middle didn't do it.

2. The dog that did do it is surrounded by at least one innocent dog on both sides.

3. The dog that did it is at least two spots away from the dog on the far left.

4. An odd-numbered dog didn't do it.

1   2   3   4   5

SOUNDS LIKE A FART

In the word search below, can you find all
the words that rhyme with fart?

```
T R A P R E T N U O C L S L S R G T N
L R R Y Q V D N Z T G H J P G M W R M
P S Q F M Q N L N P O Y R W L M A L K
N L T D L T Z N P P U N Z H R Y Y Y R X
R M T A D O D N P S T L E T R A M W T
Y T L Y T Y W I Q R W A L M P N W T N
U Y V X N E N C A D D E P A L Y W Y W
P T N K D G O K H S R Y E A P P B R J
S M Z Y C E O F T A Y Z M T R A N N K
T Z T A M G P A T N R Q X J H T R V L
A T R T A T R A Z H J T P T L E R T Z
R T A R R T P W R T E U R D D V A Y L
T T H A T R T G D T R A M L R A R R N
N Z C T I P N R Z Z H A R P M W R D T
M Q B W A Q K R A C N G E T S W D T Z
D Z Y J L G W Z E P Y K M H Z T B X Y
T J X D A X N I K T L B B R B Q A Y L
R M P Z R N P R X M T X Y Z X T N R M
N Z Y J T M Y Z J T Z D L Q R T P B T
```

Apart	Sweetheart	Smart	Martial art
Dart	Chart	Tart	Pull apart
Go-kart	Depart	Counterpart	State of the art
Jumpstart	Head start	Flow chart	Upstart
Part	Mart	Heart	
Shopping cart	Pie chart		

PICTURE PUZZLE: THOSE ARE THE RULES

This puzzle is called a *rebus*. To solve it, identify the word suggested by each image, and put them together to form a well-known (but totally unfair) "law" of farting.

Hoo! + FOREVER − 4

_ _ _ _ _ _ _ _

It

_ _ _ _ _ _ _ _ _ _

It

_ _ _ _ _ _ _ _ _

It's a Race: Get to the Farty Foods Fast!

Start at each character's name and work your way down the ladders to discover which one of the four siblings can get to each of the fart-causing foods. One thing: Every time you move down to a horizontal (sideways) line, you have to take it over to the next vertical (up and down) line and continue.

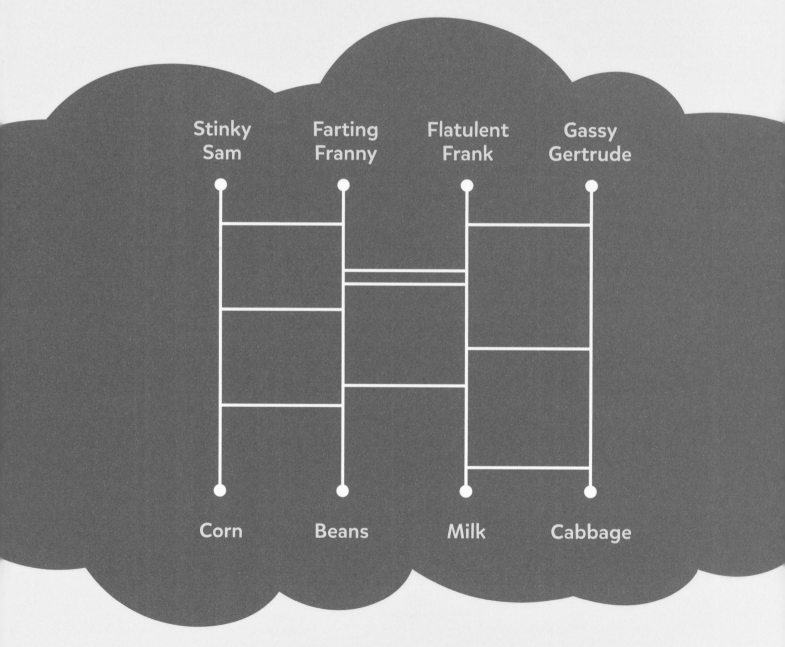

CRACK THE CODE

In the puzzle below, each number represents a different letter of the alphabet. Based on the few we've given you to get started, figure out the whole alphabet and use it to reveal a fascinating fart fact.

A	B	C	D	E	F	G	H	I	J	K	L	M
	23				9							11

N	O	P	Q	R	S	T	U	V	W	X	Y	Z
	13			10					22			

M _ _   F _ R _   M O R _
11 5 24   9 16 10 6   11 13 10 5

_ _ _ _   W O M _ _   B _ _
6 25 16 24   22 13 11 5 24   23 8 6

W O M _ _ '   F _ R _ _
22 13 11 5 24 1   9 16 10 6 1

_ M _ _ _   W O R _ _
1 11 5 12 12   22 13 10 1 5

Not Quite a Fart

There are a lot of words for farts, and then there are innocent words that just sound like they describe farts. Can you identify them and place them in this crossword puzzle?

ACROSS

1. something that burns when you start it
6. when the thing in the night sky is at its largest
7. an invisible spirit
9. an insect that smells bad
11. where you fill up a car's tank
12. when planes drop bombs
13. a large brass instrument

DOWN

1. a slip-on shoe you can wear to the beach
2. a hard to understand grumble
3. a soft, pillow-like chair
4. a light jacket
5. a gusty storm
8. something you use to flip a burger
10. a round, flat piece of bread that's soft and flaky inside

Spot the Differences

It seems that these dogs have a case of the farts. But wait: that's the same picture of the same dog! Well, *almost*. Can you spot six differences between the two pictures?

THE FART NAME DESCRAMBLER

Unscramble the following fart words. Then, the letters in the bolded boxes can be arranged to answer this riddle:

WHAT DO AN ASTRONAUT AND A HABITUAL FARTER HAVE IN COMMON? THEY BOTH _____ !

1. SASP AGS

□ □ □ □   □ □ □

2. DEIBNH

□ □ □ □ □ □

3. LFUFYF

□ □ □ □ □ □

4. KTINSS

□ □ □ □ □ □

5. TARF

□ □ □ □

6. AYSSG

□ □ □ □ □

7. OTOT

□ □ □ □

8. LTULFANTE

□ □ □ □ □ □ □ □ □

SQUARED UP: FART CLOUD

Each of four clouds can appear just once in each row, each column, and each of the four boxes. Fill in the remaining empty boxes with the pictures of each of the four fart clouds.

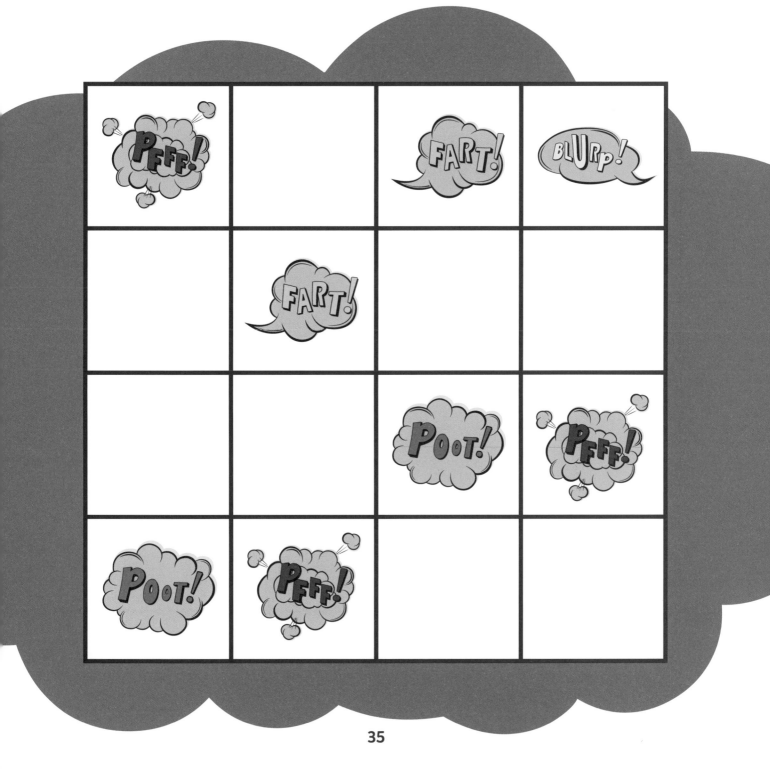

YOU CAN DRAW IT: MR. FART

Use the grid to copy the picture one square at a time.
Examine each portion of the picture of Mr. Fart in each small
square in the top grid, and then re-create those sections
in the corresponding square in the bottom grid.

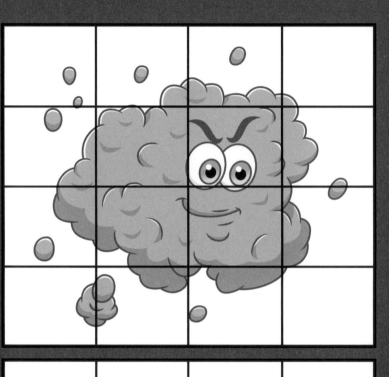

READ A-ROUND

Start at the can of baked beans. Write every third letter on the spaces until all have been used. If you place them correctly, you'll reveal the answer to this question:

WHAT DO DADS DO AFTER THEY FART?

Don't forget to cross off letters as you use them.
We gave you the first one to get started.

T___ _____ __

__ ___ ___!

THE GREAT CHILI FART FART-OFF

Two kids had chili for lunch, and now they're on the school bus sharing a seat with a third friend. Can you help the farts they've got loaded up get out . . .and reach the nose of the unfortunate person in the middle?

START

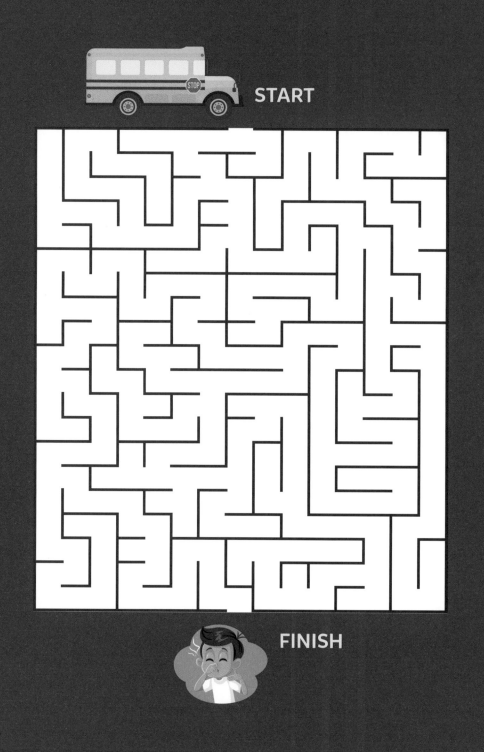

FINISH

WORD LADDER

Can you transform one fart-related word into another in just a few steps, changing only one letter each time? Answer the clues to complete the word ladder.

1. A structure kids build to play in

....

2. The thing at the end of your leg

....

3. The sound a train horn makes

....

FART

_ _ _ _

_ _ _ _

_ _ _ _

POOT

THE SPEEDING FART

According to scientists, **FARTS TRAVEL AT ABOUT 10 FEET PER SECOND.**
Based on that, can you figure out how long it would take a fart to . . .

1. ...travel from the back of a 30-foot classroom to the front?

_____

2. ...go from the back of a 40-foot school bus to the front?

_____

3. ...go from one end of a 360-foot football field to the other?

_____

4. ...reach the top of the Empire State Building? (1,454 feet)

_____

5. ...climb Mount Everest? (about 29,000 feet)

_____

HiDDEN WORD

Write the name of the fart-y food that fits on each
line (depending on how many letters it has). The bold
underlined letters, when unscrambled, will form the name
of a food that is sometimes used to mean fart.

Beans   Dairy   Lentil soup   Broccoli
Corn   Artichoke   Cabbage   Asparagus stalks

1) _ _ _ _ _ _   _ _ _ _

2) _ _ _ _ _ _ _ _   _ _ _ _ _ _

3) _ _ _ _

4) _ _ _ _ _ _ _ _

5) _ _ _ _ _ _ _ _ _

6) _ _ _ _ _ _

7) _ _ _ _ _

8) _ _ _ _ _

MYSTERY WORD:

_ _ _ _ _ _ _ _ _ _

BeFORe, AFter, IN-BetWeeN

Solve the puzzle to reveal three funny phrases—one said before a fart, one during a fart, and one after a fart. Add a letter to the empty space. Use the letters above and below the spaces, and your expert knowledge of the alphabet, to fill in the correct letter. The first one is done for you.
Note: If you get a Z, the following letter is A.

1.

Why did the truck driver stop farting?

H _ _ _ _ _ _ _ _ _ _ _ _ !

I F   S B O   P V U   P G   H B T

J G   T C P   Q W V   Q H   I C U

2.

Where does a pirate fart come from?

S G D H Q   A N N S X

_ _ _ _ _   _ _ _ _ _ !

U I   F J S   C P P U Z

3.

What's invisible and smells like bacon?

N G E   D Y P R Q

O H F   E Z Q S R

_ _ _   _ _ _ _ _ !

SAME LETTER CONNECTOR

Boxes connected by lines contain the same letter. We've given you some letters, which you can use to fill in some boxes. Others you'll have to figure out on your own. Once all the boxes are filled in, you'll find a funny—and disgusting—truth about farts.

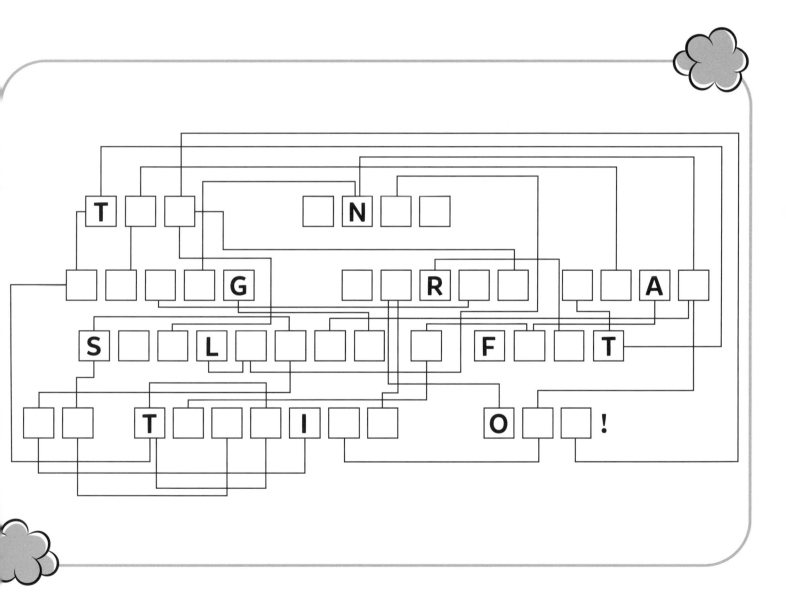

THE FARTING CROSSWORD PUZZLE

There are a lot of phrases that mean "to fart." Finish the crossword by completing the silly slang sentences.

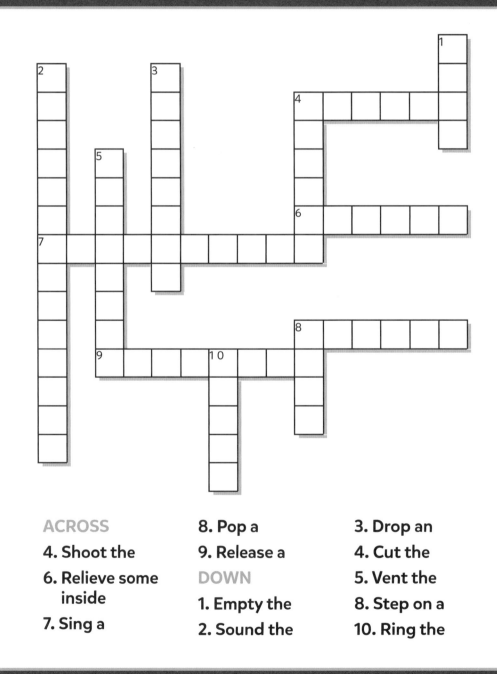

ACROSS

4. Shoot the
6. Relieve some inside
7. Sing a
8. Pop a
9. Release a

DOWN

1. Empty the
2. Sound the

3. Drop an
4. Cut the
5. Vent the
8. Step on a
10. Ring the

44

COLORFUL SCENTS

Color this pooting koala and bring her colorful farts to life.

CONNECT AND COLOR: PUNGENT FOODS

Connect the dots to complete this picture of a fart-inducing food. Fill in the blanks and add color if you know what it is!

A BAD TIME FOR A FART

Identify the worst possible places you could fart (or where you could be when somebody else farts). Use the clues to help you unscramble the words. Then take the letters in the bolded boxes and unscramble them to spell what you'd never want a fart to be.

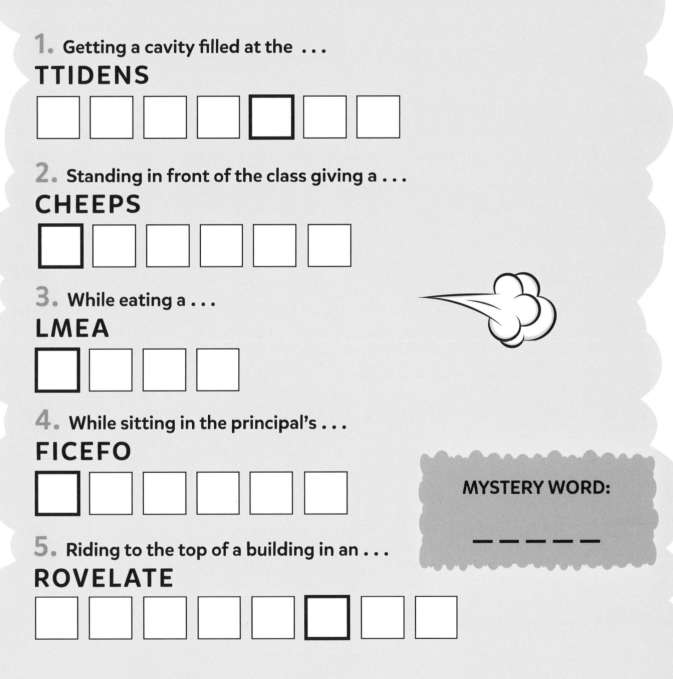

1. Getting a cavity filled at the . . .

TTIDENS

☐ ☐ ☐ ☐ **☐** ☐ ☐

2. Standing in front of the class giving a . . .

CHEEPS

☐ ☐ ☐ ☐ ☐ ☐

3. While eating a . . .

LMEA

☐ ☐ ☐ ☐

4. While sitting in the principal's . . .

FICEFO

☐ ☐ ☐ ☐ ☐ ☐

5. Riding to the top of a building in an . . .

ROVELATE

☐ ☐ ☐ ☐ ☐ **☐** ☐ ☐

MYSTERY WORD:

_ _ _ _ _

WORD SEARCH: BRINGING UP THE REAR

In the word search below, find all the words that are part of a fart's origin story.

```
S P C B R K B P N R N V V L
R T H T M R T U L Y L T Y B
E T E Y E R O B T Z Z P Y N
T B E K K R E I P T E M B X
R K K R J H E V R D O L P R
A E S R I L T I I E M C L K
U I F N A I Q S R J T U K V
Q S D A X E K M Q R J S B S
D T B E N C R O L K E Y O Y
N E L O A N S T U S H D X P
I R J B O E Y T D R N L R Y
H T M T A T A O T Q U V N W
J M J T M I Y B R R L M T Q
N K Q B L R L D W W M Q P Z
```

Backside	Derriere	Seat	Cheeks
Behind	Posterior	Buttocks	Keister
Bottom	Rear	Exit	Booty
Bum	Rump	Tail	
Fanny	Tush	Hindquarters	

PiCtURe PUZZLe: It'S a TRageDy!

This puzzle is called a *rebus*. To solve it, identify the word suggested by each image, and put them together to form a well-known poem about a disappointing fart.

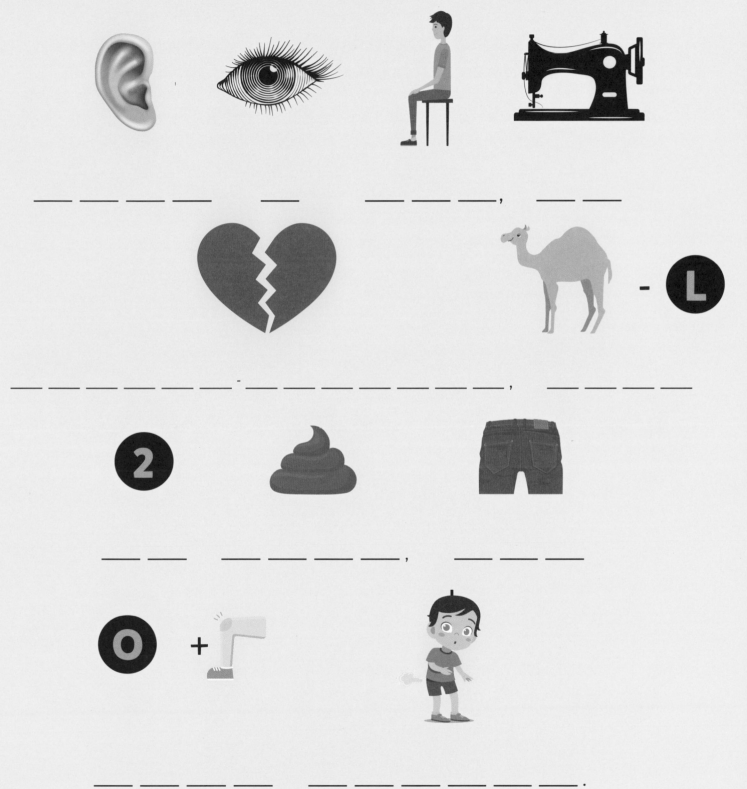

——— ——— ——— ———   ——— ——— ——— ,   ——— ——— ——— ———

——— ——— ——— ——— - ——— ——— ——— ——— ——— ,   ——— ——— ——— ———

——— ——— ——— ———   ——— ——— ——— ——— ,   ——— ——— ——— ———

——— ——— ——— ——— ——— ——— ——— .

49

RHYMES WITH "FART"

Look at the pictures and try to identify all the words
that rhyme with the subject of this book.

1.

2.

3.

4.

_____ _____ _____ _____

5.

6.

7.

_____ _____ _____

8.

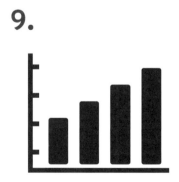

9.

10.

_____ _____ _____

BREAKFAST OF FARTING CHAMPIONS

Fuel Mr. Fart for the day ahead. Guide him to the boiled eggs and beans for breakfast!

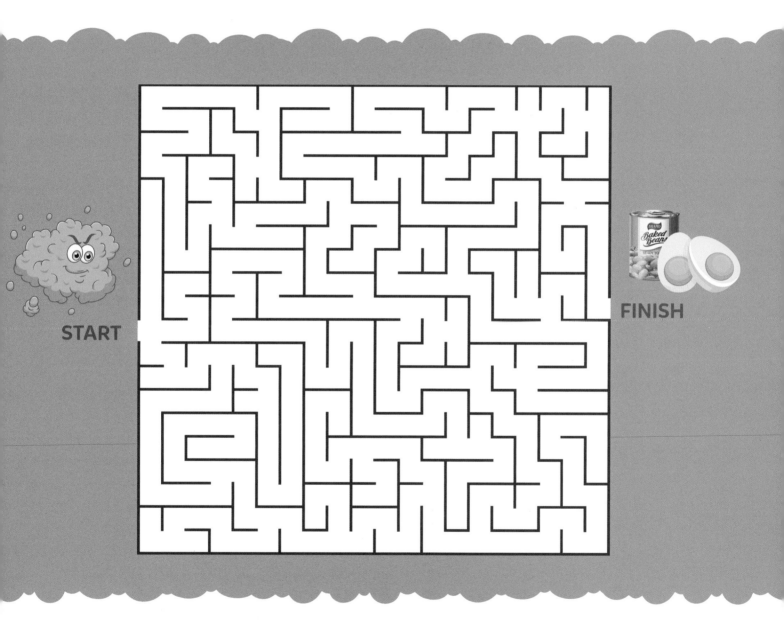

START

FINISH

CRACK THE CODE

In the puzzle below, each number represents a different letter of the alphabet. Based on the few we've given you to get started, figure out the whole alphabet and you'll get the answer to this joke:

WHAT'S THE DIFFERENCE BETWEEN AN ART GALLERY AND A CAN OF BEANS?

A	B	C	D	E	F	G	H	I	J	K	L	M
16												

N	O	P	Q	R	S	T	U	V	W	X	Y	Z
	3				14	17					13	

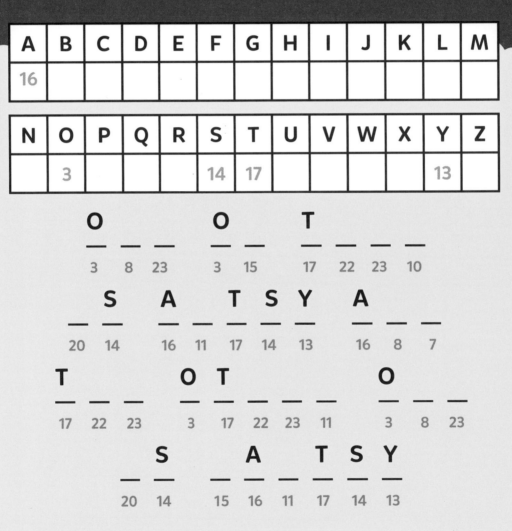

O _ _   O _   T _ _ _
3 8 23   3 15   17 22 23 10

S _   A T S Y A _ _
20 14   16 11 17 14 13 16 8 7

T _ _   O T _ _ _   O _ _
17 22 23   3 17 22 23 11   3 8 23

S _   A _ T S Y
20 14   15 16 11 17 14 13

WHO, EXACTLY, FARTED?

Down at the Fart Lab, one of the scientists farted so hard they broke the Smell-O-Meter. Can you figure out which scientist's fart was so foul?

THE CLUES

1. They're not wearing green shoes.

2. They're surrounded on both sides by other scientists.

3. They're using both of their hands.

4. They don't have short hair.

5. They're not holding plants or seeds.

SQUARED UP

The human body gets rid of more smelly things than just farts! Each of these images of four foul things can appear just once in each row, each column, and each of the four boxes. Fill in the remaining empty boxes with the correct pictures of each of the four farty things.

WORD LADDER

Can you transform one fart-related word into another in just a few steps, changing only one letter each time? Answer the clues to help you get there.

PANTS

_ _ _ _ _

_ _ _ _ _

_ _ _ _ _

_ _ _ _ _

_ _ _ _ _

_ _ _ _ _

POOTS

1. Roles in a play

2. A celebration

3. One who farts a lot is

4. Ten years after thirty

5. Army strongholds

6. Where ships dock

A CROSSWORD THAT'S FULL OF FARTS

There are a lot of words and phrases that just mean the same thing as a fart. Figure out where each expression listed on the next page goes in the crossword puzzle based on the length of the word and trial and error.

ACROSS

Zinger

Tail cutter

Breezer

Backdoor breeze

Wet one

Kaboom

Quack

Stink bomb

DOWN

Fizzler

Flamer

One cheek squeak

Bottom burp

Buster

Trouser cough

It's a Race: Farts That Can Go the Distance

Start at each character's name and work your way down the ladders to find out whose fart travels the fastest. One thing: Every time you move down to a horizontal (sideways) line, you have to take it over to the next vertical (up and down) line and continue.

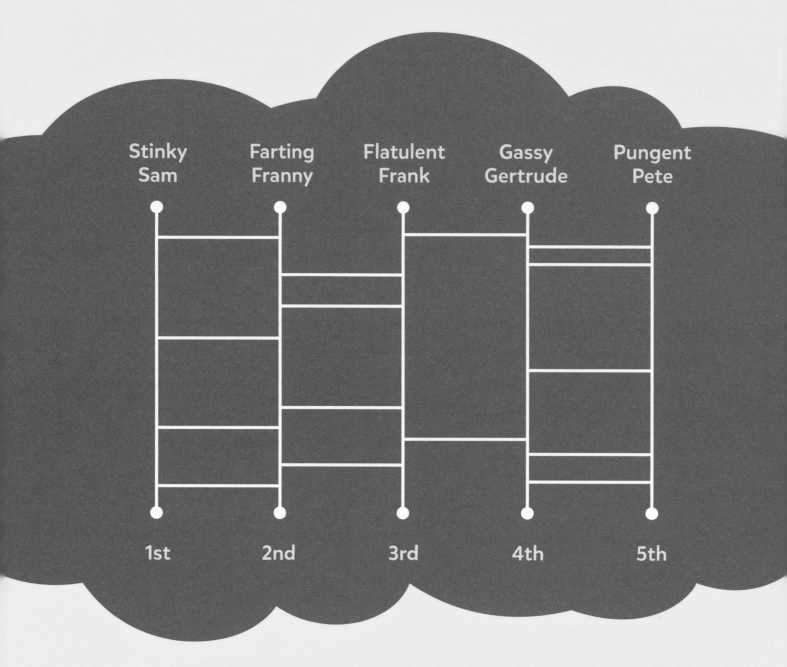

WORD SEARCH: DESCRIBE THAT FART

In the word search below, can you find all the words that you could use to describe a fart?

```
M F M L Q Y W T S Y M N Q R X N
N R M V T J L R Q K N N Y P A P
N A N W J B Q W T Q U T U S N L
P G D X T D P R T B S N T R U V
S R G N I K E E R T G Y K O N T
U A I N P K B Q I E K Y F Y R T
O N R P T G Q N X J T R Q Z
R T D A E J K T S U O I X O N M
O Y I R N Y T D R Y P K D N U Z
D L R W N C M B I X Z Y V S J J
O L T D K E I T T K Z T Q L Z
L E U G W Z T D K N E Y R R P Q
A M P G J Y R T U N R F R M M M
M S K L P T L F O T A W R Y R R
K X P R T Q Z N X R T R P J G Y
```

Rotten

Stinky

Funky

Foul

Fetid

Rancid

Putrid

Pungent

Reeking

Rank

Smelly

Malodorous

Skunky

Ripe

Musty

Noxious

Nasty

Fragrant

READ A-ROUND

Start at the can of baked beans. Write every third letter on the spaces until all have been used. If you place them correctly, you'll learn how fast farts can move out of the body and into the air.

A ____ _____ __ ____

____ ___ _____.

MR. FART'S DARING ESCAPE

Oh no, they're trying to get rid of Mr. Fart with anti-gas medicine. Help him get away as quickly as possible!

THE SCIENCE OF FARTS

The following words and phrases are all anagrams of the names of the chemicals that make up farts. Unscramble them and then use the letters in the highlighted boxes to reveal the name of a common cause of farting.

1. IRON BOXED ACID

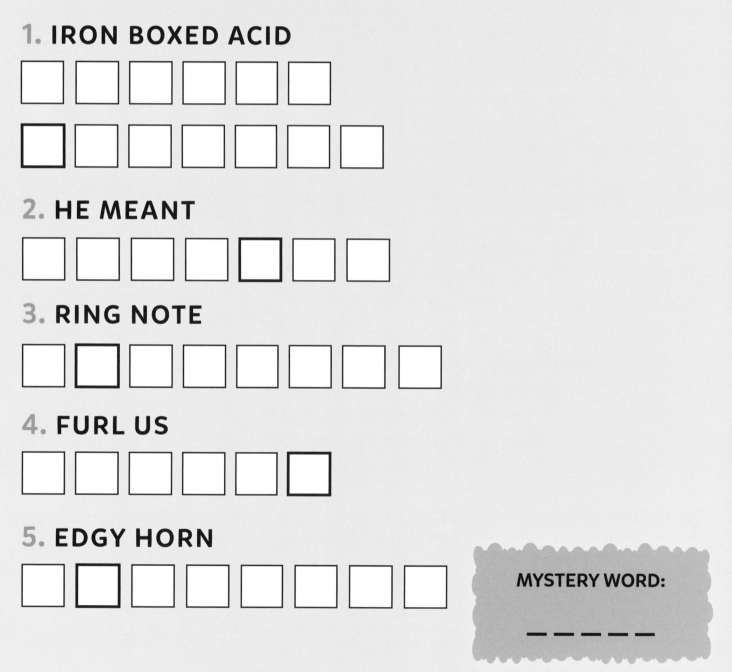

2. HE MEANT

3. RING NOTE

4. FURL US

5. EDGY HORN

MYSTERY WORD:

_ _ _ _ _

62

COlORfUl SCENtS

Color this squeaking weasel and his wild attitude toward farting!

YOU CAN DRAW IT: UNICORN

Use the grid to copy the picture one square at a time.
Examine each portion of the farting unicorn in the grid at left,
then re-create it in the corresponding square in the grid at right.

SPOT THE DIFFERENCES

It would seem that this funny kid and her twin are farting a lot. The pictures are *almost* the same, but not quite. Can you spot six differences between the two pictures?

THE FARTING CROSSWORD PUZZLE

There are a lot of phrases that mean to fart. Finish
the crossword by filling it in with the words provided.
Use the length of the words to help you.

ACROSS

Offend

Smell

Blast

Unsettle

Choke

Float

Alarm

Squirt

Linger

DOWN

Travel

Disgust

Creep

Sneak

Squeal

Attack

Prompt laughter

SQUARED UP

A fart can take on many forms! Each of four fart clouds can appear just once in each row, each column, and each of the four boxes. Fill in the remaining empty boxes with the pictures of each of the four farty things.

ODOR IN THE COURT!

One of these four people—the bailiff, the judge, the lawyer, and the defendant—farted during a trial. Act like a detective and use the clues below to find out the identity of the true guilty party.

THE CLUES

1. The guilty party doesn't wear eyeglasses.

2. The guilty party's hands are both visible.

3. The guilty party is not wearing a hat or a wig.

4. The guilty party is not between two people.

1   2   3   4

Get Away From Dad's Farts

Oh no, Dad farted in the car again, just as he pulled up to the house. Get away to safety (and fresh air) before the gas cloud catches up with you!

START

FINISH

PiCTURE PUZZLE: PANTS DANCE

This puzzle is called a *rebus*. To solve it, identify the word suggested by each image, and put them together to form a sentence you might say in response to a particularly nasty fart.

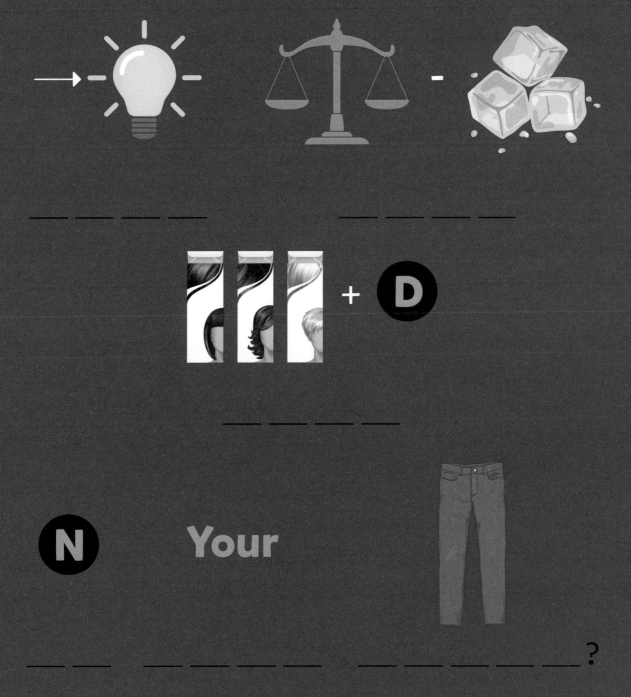

__ __ __ __ __   __ __ __ __

__ __ __ __

N   Your

__ __ __ __ __ __ __ __ __ __ __?

Not Like the Rest

Here are eight pictures of a terrible, smelly fart cloud. They all seem to be the same picture, but take a closer look. One of them is just not quite like the others. Can you find the unique picture?

1.

2.

3.

4.

5.

6.

7.

8.

WORD LADDER

Can you transform one fart-related word into another in just a few steps, changing only one letter each time? Answer the clues to help you get there.

POOT

1. A note played on a horn

_ _ _ _

2. A horse walk

_ _ _ _

3. If you spelled "fraught" like it sounds

_ _ _ _

4. Short for fraternity

_ _ _ _

5. A sweet, milky beverage minus the PE

_ _ _ _

6. A fart sound

_ _ _ _

7. An obnoxious kid

_ _ _ _

BLAT

WORD SEARCH: SOME THINGS ARE EVEN WORSE THAN FARTS

In the word search below, can you find the names of things that smell just as bad as farts?

```
M N R B T T J Y L D D R Q B V K P
O E Y R Z J M T I B N Z M V P Z J
O S A Y J K N A M K B X B T B D Q
R E R L W R P D O O F N E T T O R
H E M Q Q E L E S L Y L G W Y D N
T H P N R H R O X R E P J Z P Y S
A C I S J U T L C G E M O T D K L
B S T G N V Z A A K M W Q O C X T
G K S A N B S B E D E W E O P R Z
B U M M T U R M O R G R S S V V T
D N K I X A D L O M B O R H S I F
J K M R G G D M Y K M D D O R Y D
L O Z T P E R Y P W E V A T O W T
V J V W G L T T L Y D D N B E M P
R T J G L Q Z L V K K R B B J W Y
X D S R Y Q M Q M Z T D P D Y L W
```

Skunk	Old Eggs	Sewers	Manure
Diapers	Vomit	Wet Dog	Dung
Bathroom	Rotten Food	Armpits	Cheese
Poop	Fish	Socks	
Locker Room	Bad Breath	Garbage	

PICTURE PUZZLE:
IT'S GOING DOWN

This puzzle is called a *rebus*. To solve it, identify the word suggested by each image, and put them together to form a funny truth about farts.

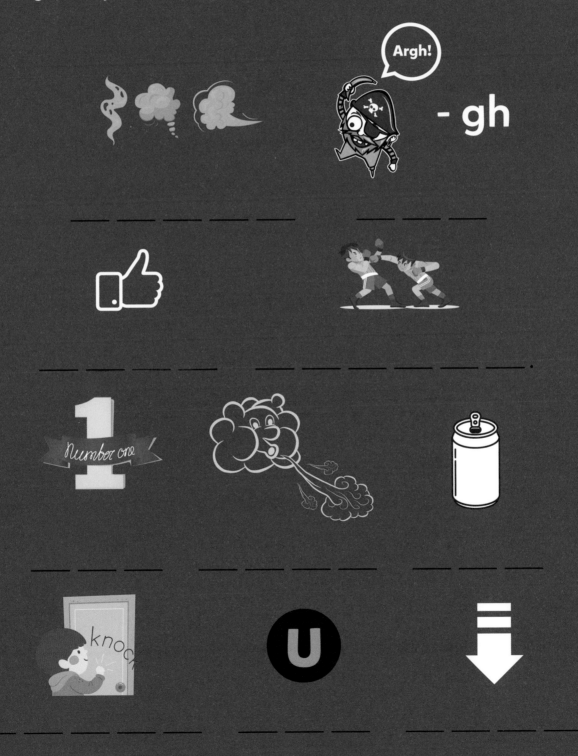

_____ _____

_____ .

_____

_____ _____ !

CRACK THE CODE

In the puzzle below, each number represents a different letter of the alphabet. Based on the few we've given you to get started, figure out the whole alphabet and you'll get the answer to this joke:

WHY DIDN'T THE FART GRADUATE FROM SCHOOL?

A	B	C	D	E	F	G	H	I	J	K	L	M
10	13		3				18				14	

N	O	P	Q	R	S	T	U	V	W	X	Y	Z

  B   **A**
___ ___ ___ ___ ___ ___ ___ ___ ___
13 23 25 10 4 9 23 17 15

H **A** **D**   **A** **L**   **A** **D**
___ ___ ___ ___ ___ ___ ___ ___ ___ ___
18 10 3 10 14 7 23 10 3 22

B   **L** **L**   **D**
___ ___ ___ ___ ___ ___ ___ ___ ___ ___ ___
13 23 23 2 23 5 20 23 14 14 23 3

76

READ A-ROUND

Start at the can of baked beans. Write every third letter on the spaces until all have been used. If you place them correctly, you'll learn about one of the benefits of being a non-stop farting machine. Remember to cross out the letters as you go.

Y_ _   _ _ _ _ _   _ _ _ _

_ _   _ _ _   _   _ _ _ _ _ _ _   _ _ _ _ _ _ _

COLORFUL SCENTS

Color this gas-emitting marsupial as she lets loose a fart for two!

FROM FOOD to FARTS

Unscramble the names of what each pictured animal's farts might smell like based on what foods they enjoy. The letters in the bolded boxes will form the name of a body part heavily involved in the release of farts.

1. SRGAS
☐☐☐☐☐

2. UPANETS
☐☐☐☐☐☐☐

3. YOHEN
☐☐☐☐☐

4. HFIS
☐☐☐☐

5. TSUN
☐☐☐☐

6. SEHECE
☐☐☐☐☐☐

7. TOAS
☐☐☐☐

8. TEMA
☐☐☐☐

9. NCRO
☐☐☐☐

MYSTERY WORD:

_ _ _ _ _ _ _ _ _

SQUARED UP

Who "nose" how to smell a fart? A nose, of course! Each fart-irritated nose can appear just once in each row, each column, and each of the four boxes. Fill in the remaining empty boxes with the pictures of each nose that work.

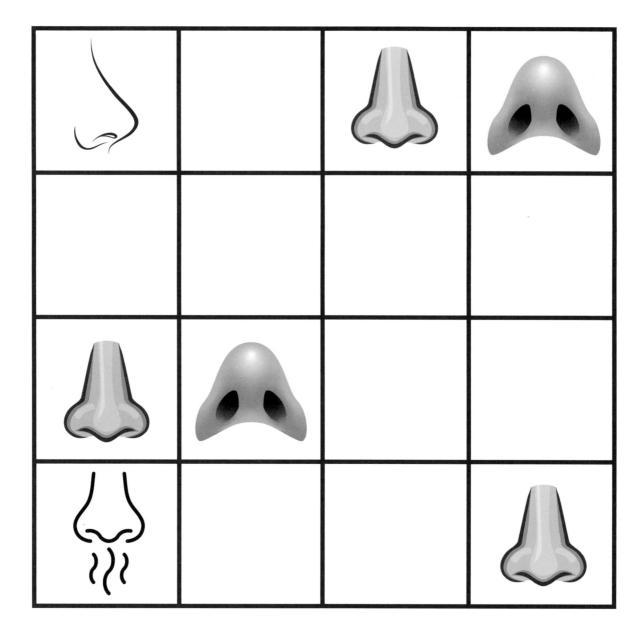

ESCAPE FROM FART ISLAND

The fart volcano on Fart Island is about to erupt. Find your way out to the boats before it unleashes the worst smell imaginable.

FINISH

WORD SEARCH: FARTING AROUND THE WORLD

Here's how to say "fart" in other countries and in languages from around the world. Can you find them all in the word search below?

```
A C R P B M P B T Q W M W
D R E R P A M R F E W Y R
A E G U I X S U U L P J Z
S P D T E Z R I T D G B N
U I R T R Z O O N Q L L B
U T O A U C T G T A P D Y
H U P A Y U N U C E D R P
D T U P M I T F O K M M B
W M Y U F N V P I Z J T T
E Y J N E L D K M S R M Y
Q Y M K Z J I L T P A L Y
```

PORDGE (Albania)

PRUD (Denmark)

PIERU (Finland)

PET (France)

FING (Hungary)

PRUTTA (Iceland)

FURZ (German)

FISA (Sweden)

PRDEC (Slovenia)

BASINA (Romania)

OCYPYY (Kyrgyzstan)

DHUUSADA (Somalia)

POEP (South Africa)

UMUT-OT (The Philippines)

A'UME (Hawaii)

KIKI (Samoa)

KENTUT (Indonesia)

CREPITU (Latin)

YOU CAN DRAW IT: CAREFUL WHERE YOU SIT

Use the grid to copy the picture one square at a time. Examine each portion of the picture of the Whoopee Cushion in each small square in the top grid, and then re-create those sections in the corresponding square in the bottom grid.

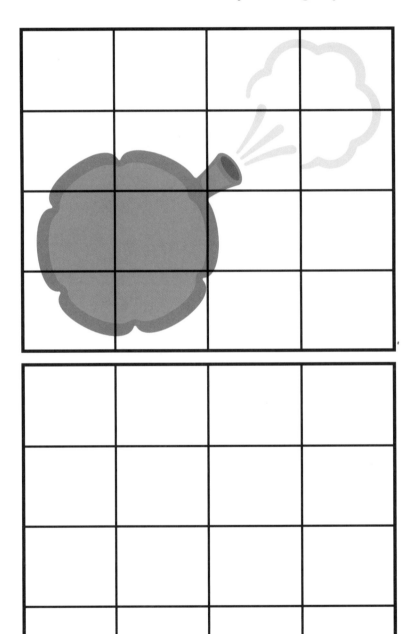

EMOJI: THE LANGUAGE OF FARTS

Here's a long and eventful story about a startling surprise and the smelly result, told almost entirely in emoji. Do your best to translate it into words below. Compare it with a friend's translation for even bigger laughs!

_____

_____

_____

_____

_____

_____

_____

_____

_____

ANSWER KEY

PAGE 4

PAGE 5

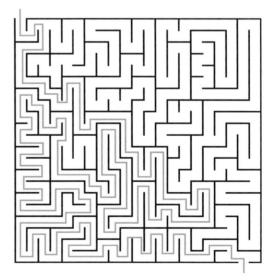

PAGE 6

Fart Rebus

Witch
One
Of
You
Cut
The Cheese
=
"Which one of you cut the cheese?"

PAGE 7

PAGES 8-9

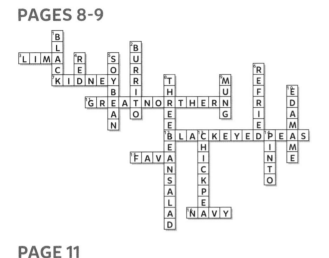

PAGE 11

Jar #4 is the one you don't want to open.

PAGE 12

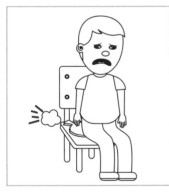

PAGE 13

Farting Franny – First Place
Gassy Gertrude – Second Place
Stinky Sam – Third Place
Flatulent Frank – Fourth Place

PAGE 14

PAGE 15

Farts you hold in during the day escape when you're sleeping.

PAGE 16

PAGE 17

One fart weighs about three ounces.

PAGE 18

1. BEAN SOUP
2. FLATULENT
3. FARTS
4. RASPBERRY
5. REAR END
6. BACKFIRE
7. STEAMER

MYSTERY WORD: BLAARRT.

PAGE 19

1. Small
2. Stall
3. Stale
4. Stare

PAGE 21

On picture #3, some extra little gas bubbles are missing.

PAGE 22

IN A REGULAR TUB, YOU HAVE TO MAKE THE BUBBLES YOURSELF!

PAGE 23

1. Pull my finger!
2. This one is silent but deadly!
3. Sorry about the gas leak!

PAGE 24

1. Yellow
2. Blue
3. Red
4. Green
5. Pink

PAGE 25

1. BOMB
2. BURGER
3. TRUMPET
4. CHEESE
5. GAS
6. WIND
7. SALUTE

The stinkiest ingredient in a fart is: methane

PAGE 27

Dog #4 is the one who released the fart.

PAGE 28

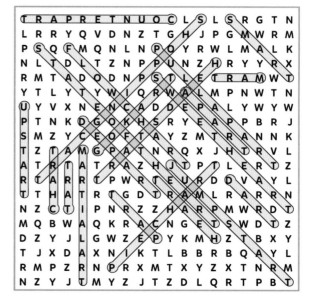

PAGE 29

Whoever
Smelt
It
Dealt
It
=
Whoever smelt it, dealt it

PAGE 30

Stinky Sam – Beans
Farting Franny – Cabbage
Flatulent Frank – Corn
Gassy Gertrude – Milk

PAGE 31

Men fart more than women, but women's farts smell worse.

PAGE 32

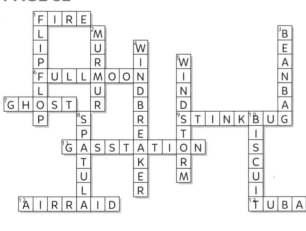

PAGE 33

PAGE 34

1. PASS GAS
2. BEHIND
3. FLUFFY
4. STINKS
5. FART
6. GASSY
7. TOOT
8. FLATULENT

Hidden word: BLASTOFF

PAGE 35

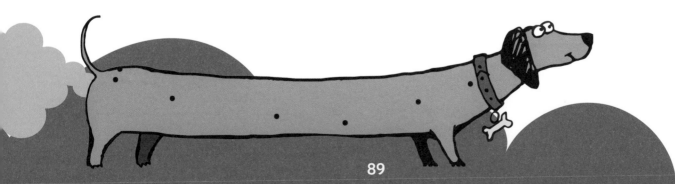

PAGE 37

They blame it on the dog!

PAGE 38

PAGE 39

1. FORT
2. FOOT
3. TOOT

PAGE 40

1. 3 seconds
2. 4 seconds
3. 36 seconds
4. 145 seconds
5. 2,900 seconds
   (just under 49 minutes)

PAGE 41

Hidden Word
1) Lentil soup
2) Asparagus stalks
3) Corn
4) Broccoli
5) Artichoke
6) Cabbage
7) Beans
8) Dairy
MYSTERY WORD: Raspberry

PAGE 42

1. He ran out of gas!
2. Their booty!
3. Pig farts!

PAGE 43

THE ONLY THING WORSE THAN SMELLING A FART IS TASTING ONE!

PAGE 44

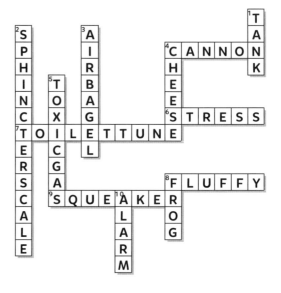

PAGE 46

It's cabbage!

PAGE 47

1. DENTIST
2. SPEECH
3. MEAL
4. OFFICE
5. ELEVATOR

MYSTERY WORD: moist

PAGE 48

PAGE 49

Ear
Eye
Sit
Sew
Broken Heart
Came
2
Poop
Butt
OH!
Knee
Farted
=
Here I sit, so broken-hearted, came to poop, but only farted

PAGE 50

1. art
2. cart
3. heart
4. tart
5. kickstart
6. smart
7. dart
8. part
9. chart
10. mini-mart

PAGE 51

PAGE 52

One of them is artsy and the other one is fartsy.

PAGE 53

It's scientist #3.

PAGE 54

PAGE 55

1. PARTS
2. PARTY
3. FARTY
4. FORTY
5. FORTS
6. PORTS

PAGES 56-57

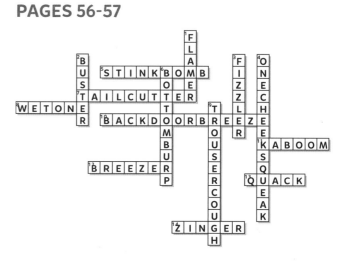

PAGE 58

Pungent Pete – First
Gassy Gertrude – Second
Stinky Sam – Third
Farting Franny – Fourth
Flatulent Frank – Fifth

PAGE 59

PAGE 60

A fart travels at ten feet per second.

PAGE 61

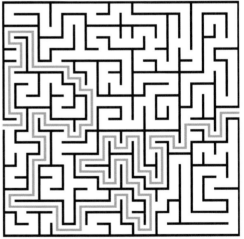

PAGE 62

1. CARBON DIOXIDE
2. METHANE
3. NITROGEN
4. SULFUR
5. HYDROGEN

MYSTERY WORD: dairy

PAGE 65

PAGE 66

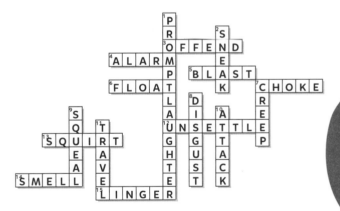

PAGE 68

PAGE 69

The defendant (#4) is guilty.

PAGE 70

PAGE 71

Watt
Justice
(−) Ice
Dyed
N
Your
Pants
=
What just died in your pants?

PAGE 72

#5 the bottom green bubbles are missing.

PAGE 73

1. TOOT
2. TROT
3. FROT
4. FRAT
5. FRAP
6. BRAP
7. BRAT

PAGE 74

PAGE 75

Farts
Argh
Like
Boxers
1
Blow
Can
Knock
U
Down
=
Farts are like boxers. One blow can knock you down!

PAGE 76

Because it had already been expelled.

PAGE 77

You never need to buy a Whoopee Cushion.

PAGE 79

1. GRASS
2. PEANUTS
3. HONEY
4. FISH
5. NUTS
6. CHEESE
7. OATS
8. MEAT
9. CORN

MYSTERY WORD: sphincter

PAGE 80

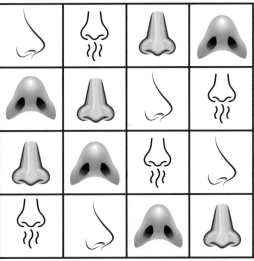

PAGE 81

PAGE 82

PAGE 85

Answers may vary, but here is one:

A kid took a flight to the United States with her mother and father to visit her grandmother in the desert. It was Thanksgiving and she was excited about the turkey dinner, bread, and pie. She drove to her grandmother's house and did not hear anything. It was totally quiet. She was confused.

She looked around. She heard a person yell and then all of her family was there, too, Surprise! She was so startled that she made a loud and smelly fart. She worried the fart was so bad that she'd also pooped. She was relieved that she hadn't pooped and had turkey and pie with her family.